my CRYPTO

Security ABC

Disclaimer:

All information provided in this handbook is intended for informational purposes only and shall serve solely to inform and raise awareness on the storage, use and cryptocurrency market entry risks that users of cryptocurrencies came across in the past.

The handbook is intended solely to provide guidance on how to act on the cryptocurrency market and how to handle cryptocurrencies. Its users shall be solely responsible to examine the circumstances of specific cases they come across.

The manual does not constitute an official document. Statutory regulations and standards shall primarily apply. As a result, the authors and publisher of the manual and other individuals involved in its creation shall not be held liable for any damage incurred by holders of cryptocurrency tokens/coins arising from abuse, thefts and other adverse activities of third parties. They shall also not be held liable for any inappropriate or improper use or interpretation of the handbook.

By using this handbook, its readers confirm that they have read, understood and consented to the General Terms and Conditions and the Disclaimer as published on https.//icryptonow.com.

My Crypto Team

Photo: Adobe Stock

Contents

Introduction 6

What should all cryptocurrency holders know? 7

Basic dictionary 8

How and where can you securely store your coins/tokens? 10

How do you correctly create your personal cryptocurrency wallet? . . . 11

How do you unlock your personal cryptocurrency wallet and find its public key or address? 13

How do you properly and securely store your password, keystore file and private key? 14

How do you securely check the balance on your personal cryptocurrency wallet? 15

How do you securely access your personal cryptocurrency wallet and exchanges? 16

How do you properly protect your exchange account? 17

How do you securely send cryptocurrency coins/tokens? 18

10 things that I know after reading this handbook 19

Appendix - General online security 20

About the authors 21

Cryptocurrency experts weigh in on the book 23

Have you already entered the world of cryptocurrencies or are you planning on entering it in the future?

If yes,

then this handbook

is the right choice

for you.

An increasing number of people are buying, using or trading cryptocurrencies which makes it that much more important to know how to use and store them in a secure manner as explained in this handbook.

Introduction

The world has been changing with the speed of light. Every single day brings about new findings and solutions that have a significant impact on our lives, which can easily include the blockchain technology that can be used in several aspects of modern-day life.

Blockchain technology has facilitated the creation of cryptocurrencies which have been on the march since the presentation of Bitcoin in 2009 and which have experienced a real boom in less than 8 years. This facilitation resulted in the creation of a parallel and decentralised financial market that exists solely in digital form but whose nominal value can be easily transferred to our material world.

At the point of creation of this handbook, the cryptocurrency market is not yet regulated, which has been reflected in practice by highly speculative investments on the one hand and vulnerability to fraud, theft and similar adverse actions on the other, which, however, do not deter people from entering it. Quite the contrary: the potential for extremely high profits has been piquing the interest of an increasing number of investors who, at least as far as our experience has shown, too frequently forget to ensure their security by lacking the required awareness or knowledge. As such, they are preyed upon by conmen and thieves or they lose their cryptocurrency coins/tokens in part or in full.

> **YOU ARE ULTIMATELY RESPONSIBLE FOR THE SECURITY OF YOUR CRYPTOCURRENCY COINS/TOKENS!**

The main purpose of this handbook is not to tell its readers in-depth on how the blockchain technology, trading, exchanges, etc. operate, but to provide basic information with a focus on security. You should consider this handbook as a driving school intended for people who want to drive along the paths of the cryptocurrency world and survive without incurring any major accidents, injuries or losses.

Since the number of cryptocurrencies and their storage options by far exceed the scope of this handbook, specific terms have been defined solely for the Ethereum blockchain used by the majority of cryptocurrencies at the point of creation thereof. However, this shall not be construed as favouritism of some or disregard for other cryptocurrencies and projects, but the selection has been made solely to prevent the handbook from overflowing from data which would have made it too long and non-transparent.

What should all cryptocurrency holders know?

If you are a holder of one of the many cryptocurrencies or are planning to become one in the very near future, tick the boxes in front of the questions that you are absolutely sure you have a great knowledge about the topic. Otherwise cross them.

- [ ] How and where can you securely store your cryptocurrency coins/tokens? **1**
- [ ] How do you correctly create your personal cryptocurrency wallet (example with MyEtherWallet)? **2**
- [ ] How do you unlock your personal cryptocurrency wallet and find its public key or address? **3**
- [ ] How do you properly and securely store your password, keystore file and private key? **4**
- [ ] How do you securely check the balance on your personal cryptocurrency wallet? **5**
- [ ] How do you securely access your personal cryptocurrency wallet and exchanges? **6**
- [ ] How to properly protect your exchange account? **7**
- [ ] How do you securely send cryptocurrency coins/tokens? **8**

Now count the ticked and crossed boxes. How many are there of each?
Our recommendation:

Even if you have ticked 8 boxes, you are still advised to read this handbook in full because it might contain additional information that you do not know.

If you have ticked less than 8 boxes, read this handbook carefully from cover to cover!

BASIC DICTIONARY

1. BLOCKCHAIN

is like **a road** on which data travel, designed in the form of a publicly accessible but fixed record that facilitates sending crypto coins/tokens from Point A to Point B.

2. CRYPTOCURRENCY WALLET

s like **a parking garage** for your cars (= stored cryptocurrency cars/tokens).
Its two essential elements are:
- your public key or address and
- your private key.

3. CRYPTO TRANSACTION

refers to **sending** crypto coins/tokens along the blockchain from Point A to Point B, whereby Point A refers to the source public key or address and Point B refers to the target public key or address.

PRIVATE KEY

s like **a key** for directly unlocking your parking garage (= personal cryptocurrency wallet). Your private key is composed of a 64-character code containing both letters and numbers. Please ensure that you store it and handle it with extreme diligence.

CRYPTO COIN/TOKEN

is like **a car** that travels along the road (= blockchain). Both terms refer to cryptocurrencies which could be, in simplified terms, referred to as electronic money.

PUBLIC KEY OR ADDRESS

is like **a unique address of your garage** that cannot be duplicated in the blockchain. All types of cryptocurrency wallets (personal wallets, exchange wallets, etc.) have one.

KEYSTORE FILE

is a coded file that **unlocks your parking garage** (= personal cryptocurrency wallet) if combined with the right **PASSWORD**.

MYETHERWALLET (MEW)

is an online service used in this handbook **as an example on how to create your personal cryptocurrency wallet** and send crypto coins/tokens.

TRANSACTION FEE OR GAS

is like **a toll** (commission) that you pay for every crypto transaction.

CRYPTOCURRENCY EXCHANGE

is like **car fair**, where cars (= crypto coins/tokens) are purchased, sold and traded.

How and where can you securely store your coins/tokens?

Under no circumstances should you store your crypto coins/tokens, that you only want to store and are not planning on using for your everyday needs (trading, transactions, etc.), in exchanges.

Online cryptocurrency wallets and exchanges are vulnerable by definition, as they are connected to a network. In addition, most private keys (and, consequently, wallets) are managed and operated by service providers of online cryptocurrency wallets and exchanges, not you.

This is why you should store your cryptocurrency coins/tokens in a so-called personal cryptocurrency wallet that transfers the ownership of the private key, responsibility for the secure handling of the private key and other access data, to you.

You can successfully avoid the risk of losing your cryptocurrency coins/tokens, stored in your personal cryptocurrency wallet, by observing tips, instructions and warnings contained in the following chapters to the T. In other words: the security of your cryptocurrency coins/tokens is dependent mostly on you and your actions.

You can also add an additional layer of security by using hardware wallets, i.e. portable standard USB devices which operate in a way that prevents access to your coins/tokens unless you have physical access to your hardware wallet. Hardware wallet definitely is a great investment (at the point of creation of this manual, Trezor and Ledger are the two most popular ones).

> Vitalik Buterin, soustanovitelj Ethereuma, je v šolskih letih računal trimestne številke dvakrat hitreje kot sošolci. Nič posebnega, v kolikor ne bi bil to razred izključno za nadpovprečne otroke. Njegov IQ naj bi na testiranjih dosegel številko 257, kar marsikoga pusti brez besed.

How do you correctly create your personal cryptocurrency wallet?

MyEtherWallet is one of the basic options for creating your personal cryptocurrency wallet.

1. Visit https://www.myetherwallet.com.

2. Select »New Wallet«.

3. Enter your desired password.

CAUTION!!! Your password cannot be changed. Forgotten passwords cannot be recovered. Make a note of your password and keep it in a secure place.

4. Press »Create New Wallet«.

5. Press »Download Keystore File (UTC/JSON)«.

Store it in minimum 2 different locations (2 or 3 separately kept USB keys are recommended).

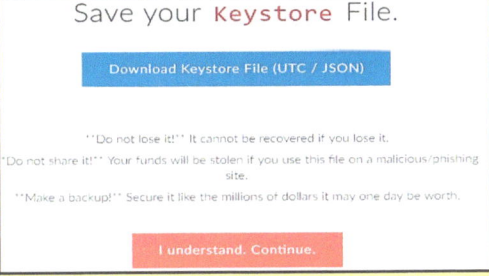

CAUTION! Under no circumstances store your keystore file in the same location as your password. DO NOT store your password in your e-mail inbox, a file on your computer or any other device with internet access.

6. If you wish to continue to saving your private key, click "I understand. Continue."

You can also do this later if you prefer. Anyone who deliberately or by accident photographs your private key, gains full access to your personal cryptocurrency wallet.

CAUTION! *Click this button only when you are alone and never in a public location where you can be seen by anyone.*

Save Your Private Key.

Print Paper Wallet

7. Make a note of your private key on a piece of paper or copy it to your Notepad and print it.

CAUTION! *Click this button only when you are alone and never in a public location where you can be seen by anyone.*

8. After your personal cryptocurrency wallet is created, make sure that you can access it easily (by logging into it, for example).

9. After you access your personal cryptocurrency wallet, you can also store its public key or address. This is the address of your crypto wallet to which crypto coins/tokens are sent.

13

How do you unlock your personal cryptocurrency wallet and find its public key or address?

1. Visit https://www.myetherwallet.com/.

2. Press »View Wallet Info«.

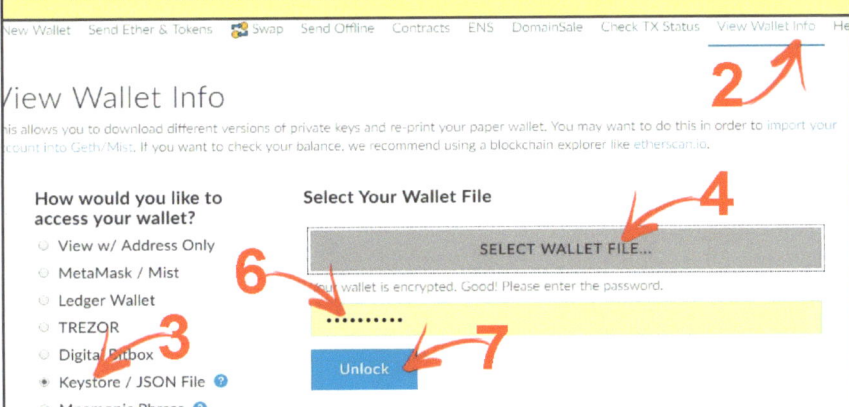

3. Select »Keystore/JSON File«.

4. Press »Select Wallet File«.

5. Find your keystore file on your USB key and select it.

6. Enter your personal cryptocurrency wallet password.

7. Press "Unlock" (which gives you access to your wallet).

8. Copy the public key (address) found below "Your Address" and save it. All public keys start with "0x...".

View Wallet Info

Your Address
0x72cCA6Fd6c5E7086CD37C25B3F99867aFE5a5E10

Public keys (addresses) can be accessed by anyone because they are public like business account numbers. You can store yours in your e-mail inbox, a file on your computer, online, etc.

How do you properly and securely store your password, keystore file and private key?

Your personal cryptocurrency wallet can be unlocked in two basic ways:

> » by using your keystore file + password or
> » your private key.

It is fundamental to store your keystore file, password and private key correctly.

Store your **keystore file** in minimum 2 different locations (your hard disk, USB key, etc.). NEVER STORE your keystore file in the same location as your password.

Make a note of your **password** on a piece of paper, Notepad or a USB key (not the same one as the one containing your keystore file) and store it in a secure location. Your password cannot be recovered or changed. Under no circumstances store your password in your e-mail inbox, a file on your computer or any other device with internet access.

Store your **private key** in minimum 2 different locations (a piece of paper, USB key, etc.). Under no circumstances store your private key in your e-mail inbox, a file on your computer or any other device with internet access.

TIP: *Public keys (addresses) can be accessed by anyone because they are public. You can store yours in your e-mail inbox, a file on your computer, online, etc.*

Checking your balance by unlocking your personal MyEtherWallet cryptocurrency wallet is not recommended because you expose the content of your wallet (coins/tokens) to risk. It is much safer to use the https://etherscan.io/ tool which does not require a log-in.

1. Type in your public key or personal cryptocurrency wallet address.

2. Press "GO" or "Enter". Your balance, including all past transactions, are displayed.

3. If you want to access the balance of any Ethereum token, click "Token transfer".

4. Use "View Tokens" to select the token of your choice.

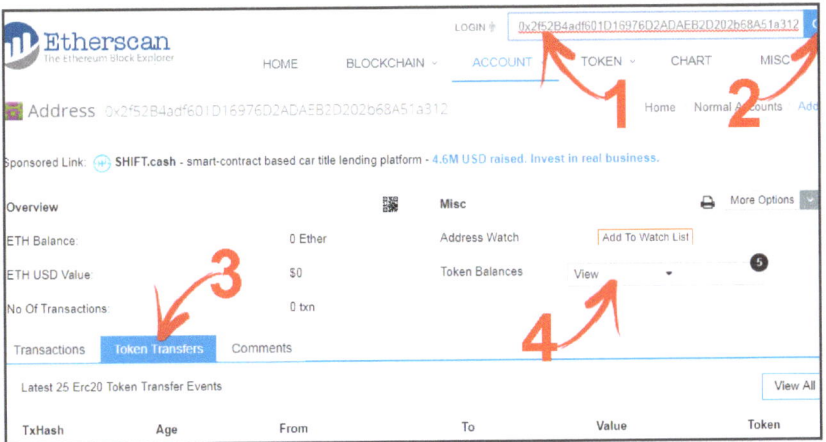

Famous athletes, film actors and Oscar winners are also excited about the blockchain technology and cryptocurrency wallets. These include soccer stars Lionel Messi and Luis Suarez, boxers Floyd Mayweather and Mike Tyson, film actor Ashton Kutcher and Oscar winner Jamie Foxx who have freely shared their involvement in the cryptocurrency world with the rest of the world.

How do you securely check the balance on your personal cryptocurrency wallet?

How do you securely access your personal cryptocurrency wallet and exchanges?

The basic rule for secure access to your personal cryptocurrency wallet and exchanges is to **never click on the search result in your search engine**. There are many "phishing" pages lurking around. Their sole purpose is to steal access data from inattentive users. Therefore, access all websites that require a **log-in directly via your saved bookmarks**.

The most common signs indicating that you have come across a "phishing" page are:

- advertised URLs,

> HitBTC Account registration | Cryptocurrency exchange market
> Oglas www.hitbtc.com/registration ▼
> Secure, support 24/7 no deposit and withdraw fee. High liquidity. Lets Trade it!

- replaced, added or missing letter(s) in the URL (Blttrex.com instead of Bittrex.com),
- replaced domain (bitstamp.com instead of bitstamp.net),
- access to the URL of the personal wallet or exchange via ads.

> *All important URLs (personal cryptocurrency wallets, exchanges, etc.) should be saved in your bookmarks and accessed only via these.*

The right URL for your personal wallet is

https://www.myetherwallet.com/.

URLs of exchanges can be accessed via

http://www.coinmarketcap.com/ under »Exchanges«.

| Cryptocurrencies: 1540 | Market Cap: $441,271,302,739 | English ▼ | USD |
| / Markets: 9115 | / 24h Vol: $17,308,712,949 / BTC Dominance: 41.6% | | |

Cryptocurrency Market Capitalizations

Install anti-virus software on the computer you use to access your personal cryptocurrency wallets and exchanges. You are advised not to use the same computer for browsing various websites that can infect it with viruses and to also make sure that it is not exposed to frequent installations of new software. For additional tips on online security, please refer to the final chapter.

How do you properly protect your exchange account?

Ensure additional security on websites where you have opened a user account which requires the use of sensitive data.

The traditional log-in with your username and password is too weak. Use 2FA (two factor authentication) to use an additional device for log-in purposes (such as your smartphone or other designated devices) which ensures additional security by ensuring that you can log in only if you are physically in the possession of the device that enables 2FA.

How do you turn on 2FA?

1. Install an application that facilitates the generation of 2FA codes on your smartphone (such as the Google Authenticator).

2. Find the option to enable 2FA in your exchange under its security settings.

3. BEFORE enabling 2FA, make a note of and securely store your recovery code that you can use if you lose or damage your smartphone.

4. Press (+) in the Google Authenticator application and select the QR code reading option.

5. Scan the QR code on the exchange website and automatically save the 2FA key onto your phone.

6. Every time you log in the exchange, enter your username, password and number generated by the Google Authenticator on your smartphone.

> The co-founder and CEO of Ripple Labs, engaged in the development of the Ripple, Chris Larsen, is deemed the richest person in the cryptocurrency world. He holds 5,19 billion Ripples. Of course, his wealth depends on the current exchange rate of Ripple whose oscillations can be measured also in billions on a monthly or even weekly level.

How do you securely send cryptocurrency coins/tokens?

You can only send coins and Ethereum tokens to your personal wallet (such as MyEtherWallet). Their public key (address) can be recognised by checking if it starts with "0x...". Before sending your coins/tokens, make sure you know on which blockchain your coins/tokens operate.

Your personal wallet has *the same public key or address* for Ethereum coins and all Ethereum tokens.

In exchanges, however, every single cryptocurrency coin/token can have its own distinct public key or address. By sending your cryptocurrency coins/tokens to the wrong public key or address, you will lose them. Irretrievably.

Coins and Ethereum tokens *are advised to be sent* as follows:

exchange -> > personal cryptocurrency wallet -> exchange

and **NOT**

exchange -> exchange.

Why? Some exchanges require the use of the first method. Always observe the proposed protocol (marked in green) to prevent the risk of loss of your coins.

TIP: To prevent errors, send a small (test) quantity of cryptocurrency coins/tokens to a specific public key or address. After your transaction is successfully confirmed and the cryptocurrency coins/tokens are received, send more. This way you will prevent loss of larger quantities of cryptocurrency coins/tokens due to a personal or technical error.

10 THINGS THAT I KNOW AFTER READING THIS HANDBOOK

I am familiar with all important basic terms associated with the storage and use of cryptocurrency coins and tokens. (pages 4 and 5) ✓

I know that I should store my cryptocurrency coins and tokens in my personal cryptocurrency wallet, such as MyEtherWallet, and, under no circumstances, in an exchange. Cryptocurrency coins and tokens should be stored in an exchange only when I intend to trade them. (page 6). ✓

I know how to create my personal cryptocurrency wallet correctly. I understand how important it is to follow the steps required to create my cryptocurrency wallet. (pages 7 and 8) ✓

I know how to unlock my wallet and find its **public key or address**. The public key can be accessed by anyone because it does not unlock my personal cryptocurrency wallet. Therefore, I can store it wherever I want and have it easily accessible. (page 9). ✓

I know that I can unlock my personal cryptocurrency wallet, such as MyEtherWallet, in two basic ways: by using my **private key** or by using my **keystore file + password**. Therefore, it is extremely important to store all of the above correctly, make a note of them and store them in a secure location. (page 10) ✓

I know that I am discouraged from logging into my personal cryptocurrency wallet to check my cryptocurrency coin/token balance. It is much safer to do that by using https://etherscan.io/. (page 11) ✓

I know that I need to use **saved URLs or bookmarks** to securely access my personal cryptocurrency wallet and exchanges. (page 12) ✓

I know that I need to ensure additional security when using exchanges by enabling 2FA (two factor authentication). (page 13) ✓

I know which steps I need to take before sending my cryptocurrency coins/tokens: I need to check on which blockchain a specific crypto coin/token operates, I need to understand that public keys or addresses are usually different for every crypto coins/tokens on exchange and know how to securely send cryptocurrency coins/tokens from one exchange to another. (page 14) ✓

I know that **I am solely responsible for the safe storage and use of my cryptocurrency coins and tokens.** However, this handbook has contributed to a greater understanding on how to securely store, send and use them. ✓

APPENDIX – General online security

Even though total security does not exist, some simple steps and responsible actions that can significantly reduce the risk of hacker attack and data theft can be taken.

Protected device access. Protect all electronic devices that contain sensitive data with a password.

Updated anti-virus software. Use only renowned anti-virus software and update it regularly.

Passwords. Use complex passwords. Use password storage and management applications or store your passwords in a secure and appropriate location, which does not have internet access.

2FA (two factor authentication). Wherever possible, access your e-mail inbox, exchanges, etc., by enabling 2FA which significantly reduces the risk of hacking the software you use.

Software updates. Update your operating system and any other software you use whenever possible to significantly reduce the risk of having your electronic devices, such as your PC, tablet, smartphone, etc., hacked.

Wi-Fi access. Never access the internet via unsecured wireless networks on electronic devices that contain sensitive data or applications.

File downloading. Under no circumstances download any suspicious files or files whose origins you are not familiar with. Do not click on any links with strange content even if you receive them from someone you know. NEVER click on .exe files unless you know who they are from and why they have been sent.

Firewall. Never switch off your firewall in your operating system and routers.

Hard disk deletion. Before disposing of or selling an electronic device, delete all hard disk data, preferably by formatting it.

The above list is by no means comprehensive and serves solely as a reminder of the security measures that can be taken by everyone.

About the authors

Grega KRAVOS

I am a teacher by profession but am also called a "multi-man", because I am an expert in many areas. I have been involved in the cryptocurrency world since 2014. As is the case with so many of us, I initially also lacked the knowledge required to overcome issues regarding the use and storage of cryptocurrencies and, as such, know very well how long it takes to learn everything that you need. When I noticed that the expansion of the cryptocurrency market also led to an increase in the number of people facing the same problems I once had to deal with, I decided that something had to be done to provide everyone with the required knowledge, explanations and instructions in one single place. This is how "My Crypto, Security ABC" came about.

Roman BERGINC

As a software developer and programmer, I regularly receive questions on processes performed on computers. I have always loved helping people. At the beginning of 2015, I became actively involved in the cryptocurrency world and noticed how much the knowledge that I could use to help others with started to expand. Because I most frequently receive technical questions that I can easily help people with, it was a no-brainer to participate in the creation of iCryptoNow because I know how much such an aid can help prevent unnecessary frustration of many cryptocurrency holders.

Jurko STARC

I have a B.A. in Economics, and have worked in IT, HR and as a librarian, although I am truly passionate about computers and the virtual world. I have amassed more than 10 years of experience in internet marketing and almost 15 years of experience in developing IT literacy programmes. I have been following the cryptocurrency world since the inception of Bitcoin and have been actively involved therein for 3 years. I believe that one of the main reasons people experience issues associated therewith is the lack of proper information. This is why I gladly joined forces with the other co-authors of the "My Crypto, Security ABC" handbook which will help provide many people with answers to many general, operational and security questions and dilemmas in an easy-to-understand and simple way.

Klemen KOLENC

I started working with people 15 years ago. Ever since the beginning, I have aimed to share the knowledge obtained at various workshops (Sales Academy, Public Speaking Master, Facebook Marketing, My Success Book, etc.) that I have attended either in person or online and which I have applied on a daily basis in my own life with as many people as possible in a simple and understandable way. As a result, I decided to participate in the creation of the "My Crypto, Security ABC" handbook whose aim is to ensure that as many users as possible know how to securely navigate the cryptocurrency world

Cryptocurrency experts weigh in on the book:

Mr. Jure Pirc,

president of the Bitcoin Association of Slovenia, independent advisor, ambassador, founder, creator, IT manager of several cryptocurrency and blockchain projects. Involved in the cryptocurrency world since 2013.

»The 'My Crypto, Security ABC' handbook is simply a must-read for everyone who wishes to become involved in the world of cryptocurrencies and Ethereum tokens because it is easy to understand even for the technically inept. How to securely store your cryptocurrencies is one of most important knowledge in crypto world, and here, this topic is very well covered on a way that can be easily understood even by the elderly. Therefore, I would highly advise you to make reading it one of the first steps you take before entering the cryptocurrency token world.«

Mr. Mitja Glavnik,

founder of Kriptovalute.si (Cryptocurrencies.si), licensed insurance agent and stock broker (A, B and C), freelance financial advisor, professional lecturer.

«The authors of the book provide you with an extremely concise illustration on how to face cryptocurrency storage risks, an affable and easy-to-understand introduction to the cryptocurrency world and practical guidelines on how to ensure sufficiently secure storage of your cryptocurrency assets. Highly recommended«.

Mr. Gašper Kenda,

creator and founder of the Xaurum cryptocurrency, software developer and programmer, involved in the cryptocurrency world since 2013.

»One of the best things I have come across recently. What an enjoyable read. The content is presented in a truly transparent and simple way. One of the main things that stands out for me is that this handbook was neither written nor designed over night because its interesting and fun content was prepared with great care, ensuring that it provides the reader with high-quality information. I would definitely recommend it to everyone who is not completely sure how to remain completely secure in the cryptocurrency world.«

Photo: Adobe Stock

www.ingramcontent.com/pod-product-compliance
Lightning Source LLC
Chambersburg PA
CBHW040311220526
45473CB00002B/634